AKELLO MARO TIMO NGO?
What does Akello love to do?

Written by Dr. Sarah Eyaa
Illustrated by Titansign

First Published 2022
Copyright © 2022

All Rights Reserved. No part of this book may be reproduced, distributed, stored in a retrieval system, or transmitted in any form or by any means without the prior written permission of the author, except in the case of brief quotations embodied in critical reviews and certain other noncommercial uses permitted by copyright law.

ISBN - 978-0-6454427-0-0

Dedication

This book is dedicated to my family and all people who are seeking to learn a local language.

This book belongs to

_____
_____

Rwatte kede Akello

Akello obedo atin nyako ame yaa iyi kaka Lango. Kaka Lango yaa iyi tung malo me Uganda dang oloko Leb-Lango. Buk-ki nyuti wa ngo ame Akello maro timo.

Meet Akello

Akello is a little girl from the Lango tribe. This tribe comes from Northern Uganda and speaks a language known as Leb-Lango. This book shows us the things that Akello loves doing.

Akello maro tuku kede ominere Obua
(Akello loves playing with her brother Obua)

Akello maro limo aba adwong kede atat
(Akello loves visiting her grandfather and grandmother)

Akello maro kwano buk
(Akello loves reading books)

Akello maro myel
(Akello loves dancing)

Akello maro goyo cal
(Akello loves drawing)

**Akello maro ngwec
(Akello loves running)**

Akello maro wot iyi cuk kede mama
(Akello loves going to the market with her mother)

Akello maro yito yen
(Akello loves climbing trees)

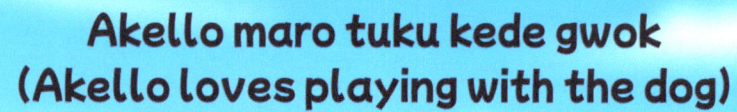

Akello maro tuku kede gwok
(Akello loves playing with the dog)

Akello maro bwonyo
(Akello loves smiling)

Yin kono, imaro timo ngo? Wek agen ni yie yom me kwano ngo ame Akello maro timo.

(What do you love to do? I hope you enjoyed reading about what Akello loves to do.)

The End

www.ingramcontent.com/pod-product-compliance
Lightning Source LLC
Chambersburg PA
CBHW041428010526
44107CB00045B/1539